MARTIN WILLIAMS AND KELLY SHEILS

101 Mindfulness Games For Happy Minds

For Children Aged 3-7

First edition

This book was professionally typeset on Reedsy.
Find out more at reedsy.com

Contents

1

About The Authors

Martin Williams

Martin Williams is the founder of the training company Early Impact. He has worked in early education in the UK for ten years, teaching children between the ages of 3 and 5. He is driven by a determination to make early learning exciting and engaging for both children and adults.

In his work with Early Impact, he has trained thousands of teachers and practitioners in many of the key areas of education. He has delivered school improvement projects for authorities, and he has led training for local early years quality teams.

He blogs and writes about all the educational topics he believes he can make a difference in, and he is strongly committed to sharing information and helping others as much as he can. You can find his blog by going to earlyimpactlearning.com

He is passionate about the 'practical' nature of learning both for adults and children. All of his courses are fast-paced, interactive, and contain a multitude of real-life resources that attendees try out.

He runs hands-on training courses in face-to-face venues across the North of England and the Midlands, specialising in early phonics, mathematics, fine motor and mark-making.

He delivers popular online training sessions through Early Impact's website which you can find here - earlyimpactlearning.com/online-courses/

Kelly Sheils

Kelly has worked in the early years for 22 years.

For more than a decade she was the Quality Manager at a large chain of private nurseries, overseeing standards of provision across the settings. She secured and maintained numerous outstanding OFSTED judgements across the chain over many years.

Kelly is a passionate level 3 Forest School Practitioner, as well as a Level 3 Tutor in teaching and training adults. She is a Relax Kids coach, offering mindful sessions to children in her local area.

Kelly has knowledge across the whole early years sphere, and specialises in Mindfulness and Mental Health, Outdoors and Forest School, and her exceptional knowledge of OFSTED and current best practice.

Kelly leads Early Impact's inhouse sessions 'Wellbeing And Mental Health Bootcamp' and is the co-creator or our online course 'Happy Minds Academy' which you can find here - https://earlyimpactlearning.com/happy-minds-academy/

2

Your Free Book

Your Free Book Is Waiting

How do you get children excited about numbers when playing outside? How can you inspire outstanding progress in mathematics through outdoor learning? How can you set up engaging activities on a limited budget?

This beautifully illustrated book provides 50 inspirational number activities for children aged 3 to 6.

Download '50 Outdoor Number Activities On A Budget' Free At This Link Below

https://earlyimpactbooks.com/50-games/

Download for free at – https://earlyimpactbooks.com/50-games/

3

A Time For Mindfulness

Modern education can be really overwhelming.

It works a bit like an unstoppable steam-train. Children are propelled at maximum speed through a set of experiences, activities, and learning intentions.

Children are bludgeoned with activity after activity...

....objective after objective...

...they are surrounded by others wherever they go...

...there is so much happening every minute, every second.

There is, however, lots of research that shows that changing up this tempo of experience has many benefits. Introducing moments of calm and restfulness helps children to process what's just happened. It's helps them to think and to reflect on their learning.

These are the moments that make up many of the games in this book. They are moments of reflection, meditation, calm, and of learning how our minds work, how our bodies work, and how to create a deeper connection with the world around us.

And here is the bottom line - introducing mindfulness into your setting can massively enhance learning.

Mindful children are more relaxed, and their brains will be operating closer to their full potential. They will be able to relate fully to the present, give their whole attention to events, and be generally healthier and happier.

However, to rewind slightly to start with, what exactly is mindfulness? And how does it work in education?

There are many ways of looking at mindfulness from an education perspective, all of which feed into each other. Some of these include:

It Is About Being Present

Mindfulness helps us to be more strongly connected to the *here and now*. Not focussing on the past or future so much helps to relieve anxiety and stress. It also makes you more 'in control' of your life, as the present is the only thing you can impact.

It Is A Way Of Training Your Mind

Mindful practices help to discipline and sharpen our mental processes.

It Is A Relaxation Technique

Mindfulness helps both our brains and our bodies to relax. This helps everything function far more efficiently.

Giving Complete Attention To Things

This is an especially massive thing in the modern world. Mindfulness teaches us to take on one challenge at a time, and fully focus on whatever it is you are doing.

In many ways, mindfulness underpins and enhances all learning. In particular, some of the main benefits of mindfulness in education include some of the following:

- The resources required are either free or extremely cheap
- It stimulates progress across the whole curriculum
- It has an holistic impact on the whole child
- It positively impacts physical health
- It helps develop a positive mental attitude
- It supports good mental health
- It is a skill that can be used for life

That then, in a nutshell, is what mindfulness is, and the huge benefits it can have on children.

But now for the tricky bit - how to actually make this happen in the real world!

That is where the rest of this book comes in. Mindfulness is very much a practical thing, and this book takes a very practical approach. The best way to explain mindfulness is to demonstrate what mindful games and activities actually look like.

Mindfulness is meditating...it is yoga...it is deep breathing...it is learning how to fully engage our minds...and, very importantly, it is a way of deeply embedding learning.

It is all these things, and so many more, but the biggest challenge is what on earth this all looks like when children are doing it.

Ask children to breathe deeply, and they will probably all smirk!

Tell them to lie on the floor and meditate and they will be laughing hysterically.

But magically weave these things into games, and pretence, and role-play, and make-believe, and you will have children breathing and meditating, and engaging in so many other mindful practices before you know it.

This book brings mindfulness to life in all its core components. The big thing is to make it fun, make it a game, and bring it to life in any way you can.

Mindfulness is not an add-on to the curriculum. It can be a daily practice of games and activities that can easily be 'thrown in' to the rest of the things that you are doing. These games are often quick, fun, simple, and require no preparation. They will help children be more relaxed, be able to think better, and be able to make more substantial progress in learning across all areas.

We have broken this book up into many key parts of the curriculum, and described many of the best games to teach mindfulness in these areas. These activities are road tested...simple...inspirational...and most importantly - they work!

Many of the games may surprise you.

For example, there is a whole chapter about mindfulness and vigorous physical movement, and how the two can go hand in hand.

So, it's time to relax, and become fully absorbed in our journey through the best 101 mindfulness games for happy minds.

4

Breathing Games

Why is breathing such a big deal in mindfulness?

There's actually a few reasons. Breathing has many positive effects on our minds, and also on the ability to learn. All-in-all, something as simple as breathing can have a massive impact.

In school or childcare settings, children are continually surrounded by many others.

This has many good aspects, but there are also a few negative side-effects.

Overwhelm is a massive one. Children can become over-stimulated as there's just so much going on all the time.

There is also often going to be some conflict and things going wrong, and this is exacerbated by the number of people around you. Children are wrapped up in an environment of activity, flux, and challenge.

So, where does breathing come in?

When we are stressed or anxious, our breathing becomes quicker and more shallow.

This originates from the 'flight or fight' instinct. Stress increases adrenaline, which increases the speed of breathing.

Many children are partly in this 'flight or fight' state for a large proportion of their lives. In this state you have less control over the way you think and the way you act.

Believe it or not, probably the quickest way of releasing children out of this state is deep breathing.

Long and slow breathing has a calming effect.

It reduces stress.

It actually helps us think much more clearly and get back that element of *control* that is often lost when we are entering into a 'flight or fight' state.

But the thing is, teaching breathing techniques to children is very different to doing it for adults.

It works best if it is fun!

It also works well if there is some element of make-believe, or imagination, and that the whole thing is turned into a game.

One thing that is great about all of the following games is that they are quick. They can be thrown into your busy day to provide moments of calm, and regeneration.

Here, then, are some of the very best breathing games...

1. Bunny Breathing

A nice and simple idea to warm up with. The children are all now bunnies, and they are going to be sniffing the air (the way rabbits do).

Encourage the children to put their noses into the air and take lots of quick sniffs in through the nose, and then a long breath out through their mouth.

This easy idea is a way of getting them to regulate their breathing in a fun and imaginative way.

2. Teddy Breathing

Some kind of toy is required for this game.

It could be a teddy bear, or whatever other toys you have to hand will be fine.

The children all have one cuddly toy each, and they lie down with it on the floor. They try to balance the toy on their chest, and they are going to watch it as they lie still.

Teddy Breathing

The teddy (or toy) will be rising up and down with their chest as they breathe in and out.

This is a brilliant game for breath control. If you breathe more deeply, the toy will move up and down in more exaggerated movements. Breathe more shallowly, and it moves less.

Some suggestions you can make to the children are:

i) Try to hold your breath for a few moments so the toy is still

ii) Try to move it up and down quickly by breathing rapidly. They often find this quite funny which can lead to the next idea...

iii) See what happens when you laugh

iv) Use really slow deep breaths. These are great for calming children down, whilst also focusing their attention on the toy (a double effect).

3. Breathing Out Colours

There is a psychological link between colours and feelings.

For example, blue and grey are often associated with sadness. Yellow is often associated with sunlight and happiness.

Of course, not all people have the same emotion associated to a colour. However, being able to imagine a colour and then 'breathe it out' can provide a sense of empowerment and control.

What you do is this – ask the children to think of a colour that makes them happy.

Then get them to close their eyes, and take a deep breath in through their nose. As they breathe out, imagine that the room is filling with that colour. Keep breathing out, and filling the room with the colour.

An easier way to do it is to suggest the colour. For example, pick a colour like red. The children close their eyes, and breathe out the colour red, filling the room.

This is a beautiful visualisation activity, where children get to imagine their control over the world.

4. Feather Breathing

This is a really simple breathing game, that is good even for young children to attempt.

You need at least one feather per child to start with. A bag of coloured feathers is perfect for this (the kind you might get in an arts and crafts shop).

Bags of colourful feathers can be picked up really cheaply from arts and crafts stores

Demonstrate how to do it first. Take one feather and place it in your hand. Then inhale, and breathe out onto the feather, blowing it out of your hand. It's that simple!

The children all take a feather and then try to blow it out of their own hands.

The next step is a bit trickier. Put the feather back on your hand, inhale and then try to blow out in a really gentle way, so that the feather doesn't fall off your palm. You will see the feather rustling slightly, but hopefully not flying off.

This game really helps them to control and calm their breathing.

5. Whistle Breathing

A whistle is probably the simplest wind instrument that children can try out.

For this activity, you need one whistle per child. You can normally buy packs of whistles really cheaply. It's probably an activity you can only do once, unless you sterilize the whistles (which is definitely an option). If you do it just once, you can always send the whistles home with the children at the end. The parents will love you for this, we promise you (big wink!).

There are lots of games you can try with the whistles, all of which really help children to control their breathing.

Outdoors is probably best for this, and just be careful not to really upset the neighbours.

Demonstrate how to use the whistle, and then give them out. The children can experiment with blowing into it to start with.

It's good to have some kind of 'stop!' hand signal, so children know when to stop blowing. Practise this, and be firm!

Demonstrate how to experiment with different types of noises.

You can:

i) Try to make a really quiet noise
ii) Make a really loud noise! (hold your ears)
iii) Make a wobbly noise
iv) Make a fast succession of noises
v) Go quiet-loud-quiet-loud in crescendos and diminuendos

6. Take 5 Breathing

This is a beautiful mindful finger play that is great for practising breathing.

Put your hand out and spread the fingers out wide.

Then, with the index finger on your other hand, slide up one finger and down the other side.

As you slide up a finger, breathe in through your nose. As you slide down, breathe out through your mouth.

Keep going with different fingers.

A great way to focus their attention, and calm things down as well.

7. 'My Magic Breath' Book

There are several good quality mindfulness books for young children, but definitely the number one go-to guide is 'My Magic Breath' by Nick Otner and Alison Taylor.

This book is a fantastically interactive experience, with the children able to breathe along in different ways as it is read to them.

It gives children the magical tool of breathing to find calm in the busy world we live in.

8. Imaginary Bubbles

This is a kind of group role-play activity.

Like many of the best mindfulness games, absolutely no resources are required.

The children are going to imagine that they will blow bubbles. They have an imaginary pot of bubble mixture in their hand and a pretend bubble wand.

They put the wand to their mouths and blow 'bubbles'. It is all about visualising the bubbles as you blow them, and experimenting with all the different types you can create.

This is another excellent game for controlling breathing.

Some ways the children can blow bubbles include:

i) Blowing really big bubbles, with long controlled breaths
ii) Blowing lots of little bubbles, with rapid breaths
iii) Blowing in different directions

You can add some moments of pause and calm, visualising the bubbles flying out of the window and sailing away through the sky.

9. Balancing

This is a slightly trickier mindfulness game. It is great for children that like building with blocks.

It is good to try as a pairs game.

One child is going to lie on the floor, facing up.

The other child is going to have a few wooden blocks. They are going to try to build a small tower of blocks on the other child's body.

Somewhere like the chest or belly is a good place to start.

The child lying down must try to control their breathing so the tower doesn't fall.

When they have tried building a tower for a few minutes, then swap roles, and the other child has a go of building.

There are many ways of adapting this game, such as:
i) Build on different parts of the body, e.g. on the back of the hand, or on the back (if the child is lying face down)
ii) Play the game sat up, not lying down
iii) Try to build a tower on your own body

10. One Nostril Breath

This is another child-friendly way of experimenting with a fun way of breathing. It draws attention to how we breathe, and also helps to control it.

It's very simple this idea – children put a finger over one nostril, breathe in through the other one, and out through their mouth.

They repeat this a few times, and then switch over to put their finger on their other nostril.

11. Bumble Bee Breathing

First, demonstrate what a bumble bee hum sounds like - hmmmm. The children enjoy humming like this, and it is great for speech and language skills, and early phonics (as well as all the super mindfulness benefits).

The idea of this activity is that the children breathe in silently through their noses, and then breathe out whilst making a hum with their mouths (like a bee).

After they have had a go of doing this a few times, get them to put their hands over their ears as they breathe out. This makes them aware of vibrations through their head.

5

Interacting Mindfully With The Elements - Earth, Water And Air

This chapter demonstrates how simply children can be encouraged to interact with the world around them.

By looking, feeling, and deeply engaging with simple things like the wateriness of water, or the colour of the sky, children learn about the world and also about themselves.

1. Send Bubbles To Space

Bubbles can be extremely exciting! But they can also be calming.

'Send bubbles to space' is an activity that helps children observe and reflect.

The idea is to have some kind of bubble mixture and wands. Something like little pots of bubble mixture would be great. You could also use homemade bubble mixture and some other kinds of larger wands. The larger ones are particularly good for younger children.

This game works well on a day when there is a little bit of wind.

Blow bubbles up into the air, and watch them float away. Many will drop to the floor, but some will travel upwards.

The focus of the activity is watching as some sail away. Where are they going? Space?

This game generates talk, and also is an exciting way to get the children watching and thinking.

2. At One With Water

Water has many calming properties.

Simply experiencing the 'wateriness' of water has many benefits.

As a simple adult-led activity you can try, ask children to put their hands into a trough of water. Try some of the following things:

i) Put their hands on the bottom of the tray and leave them there. What does the water feel like on their hands and arms?

ii) Make ripples in the surface with their fingers

iii) 'Poke' the water and watch the circular ripples

iv) Swish the water around, and make small waves

v) Part your fingers, and lift them out of the water. How does the water drip from your hands?

vi) Cup your hands and lift them upwards filled with water. What happens?

vii) How long can you hold a handful of water before it disappears?

3. Cloud Gazing

Clouds are a kind of magic show in the sky.

On many days they are continually moving, appearing and disappearing.

You have clouds of so many textures and colours – fluffy, white, floating, feathery, woolly, wispy, misty, foggy, gloomy, black, stormy, red, and pink (to name just a few).

Teaching children to 'look' at clouds and not just take them for granted is a big step. It is a good way of helping them to really observe the world around them, and find feelings of gratitude and wonder.

On a day when there are clouds in the sky, ask them to lie on their backs and look upwards. You could provide blankets, or something similar, to lie on.

Try some of these things:

i) Can you see any pictures in the clouds?
ii) What do they look like?
iii) Where are they going?
iv) Where have they come from?

Other cloud activities include:

i) Representing them in pictures or art

ii) Take photos of them with ipads or something similar

iii) Explore different filters or effects with photos

iv) Link the clouds you see to pictures in books (for example a science book with different types of clouds – cumulus, cirrus etc)

4. Zen Garden Small World

Japanese Zen Gardens are places of tranquillity and contemplation.

The idea of a Japanese Zen Garden is that it is a miniature representation of nature. This kind of garden might have rocks in it that are shaped like mountains, a water feature like a river, bushes for trees, and so on.

You can create miniature Zen Gardens in a multitude of ways, including:

Small World Zen Gardens

Fill the inside of a tyre or large plant-pot with sand. Add some pebbles, petals, leaves, and anything else like that.

Add some small figures for the children to play with, and then you have a Zen Garden backdrop for imagined role-plays.

Children Make Their Own

Each child has a tray or a plate for this. They need a supply of sand, rocks and petals (and whatever else you have to hand).

They cover the tray or plate in sand, and add rocks, petals and whatever else.

Zen Gardens have ripples in the ground, signifying the movement of water.

The children can have a go of creating this in the sand using a craft stick or a fork to swirl it around.

A small Zen Garden in a tray with sand and a few other resources

Set Up A Reflection Space

If you have a bit of time, a small budget, and a space you can use, setting up a large Zen Garden as a reflection space could be a real possibility for you.

As a minimum, you'll need lots of bags of pebbles, a few large rocks, some small bushes, and some simple and natural seating for the children.

Check out some Youtube videos of how this is done on a very conservative budget.

5. Mindful Stones

Many children have a natural fascination for stones. They are simple and unique treasures that you can find all over the place.

Encourage the children to go on a hunt to find their perfect stone. Some kind of environment where there are at least a few stones on offer is required for this (obviously!).

When they have found them, encourage them to look at their stone and those of others. What do they look like? Feel like? What colour are they? What weight are they? etc

The children can paint or draw images on their stone.

You can then do any of the following:

i) Bury the stone for others to find

ii) Place them all in a jar in the setting that the children have access to

iii) Integrate them into small-world play

iv) Use them for simple circle times. Children hold their stone, give their ideas one at a time, and then place their stone in a basket

Painted mindful stones

6. The Flowing Of Water

This is a very open-ended activity.

To experience the flow of water, you can use any of the following:

i) Gutters
ii) Funnels
iii) Pipes
iv) Large bamboo tubes

Children can experiment with all of these. They can also use a range of loose parts to travel and float in the water. Some good examples could be:

i) Corks
ii) Leaves

iii) Sticks
iv) Balls
v) Stones

This is an activity where the process and the experience of how water works is the most important thing.

7. Puddle Potions

There are so many things you can do with puddles!

Something as simple and as beautiful as floating petals in them will really spark children's curiosity.

Puddle potions

Children can also poke and swirl the puddles with their fingers, exploring the ripples.

Potions are one of the ultimate puddles activities. For this, the children can just gather whatever 'ingredients' they can find outside.

They can, for example, put leaves, petals, and grass into the puddles. You can stir it around with sticks, or with wooden spoons.

Potions can be created first in a pestle and mortar and then added to the puddle.

Pestle and mortars are great for creating spooky concoctions

8. Leaf Boats

Leaf boats are quite simply leaves floating in a puddle.

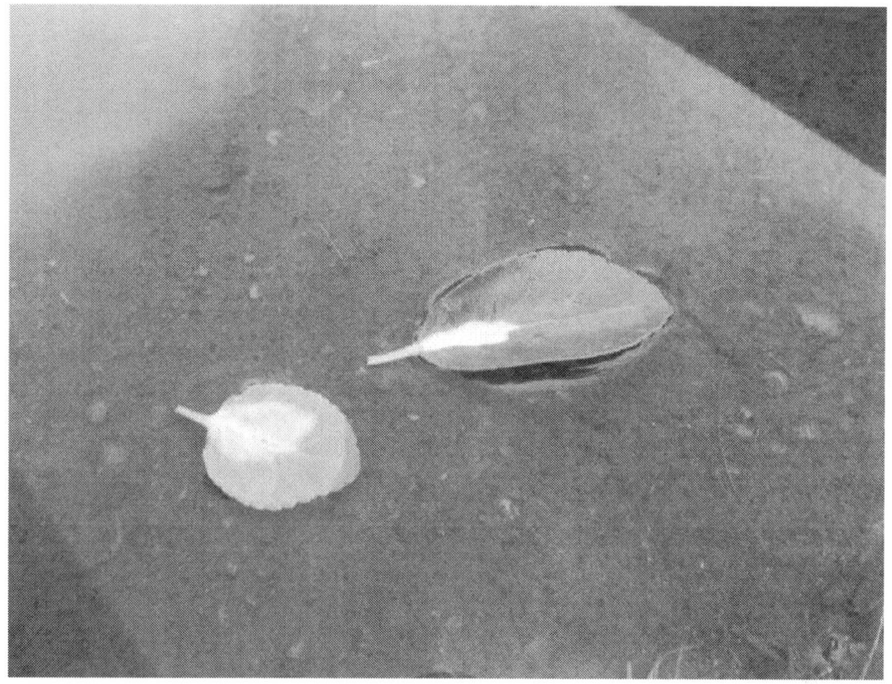

All aboard the leaf boats

Find some leaves that you think will do the job. You can also balance some things on these leaves, such as pine cones, petals, grass, tiny pebbles, or whatever else you find.

Place whatever it is on the leaves, and then launch the boats. Watch them sail around the puddles.

You can create ripples with sticks or your finger.

9. Nature Photography

Photography is really accessible for children nowadays.

You can use simple apps on tablets or ipads, or have a go of child-friendly cameras.

Of course children love taking selfies and pictures of their friends. However, for mindfulness the trick is to teach them how to take photographs of their environment.

Doing this adult-led first is the way to go, and then they can hopefully later try it more independently.

Doing a kind of group photography trail is a good way to start. Have a go of taking pictures of the same subjects together.

Some examples of great things to take photos of include:

i) The bark of trees
ii) Flowers
iii) Plants
iv) Squirrels, birds, or any other animals they find
v) Bugs
vi) The clouds
vii) Rocks or stones
viii) Wooden tables

Taking photos and later examining them strengthens their appreciation of all the things they are looking at. It gets them really looking at what is around them.

6

Child-Friendly Yoga

There are several studies that have shown the benefits of children doing yoga. Amongst them are:

i) Aiding flexibility
ii) Developing strength
iii) Developing an inner calm
iv) Relaxing the mind so it is better able to learn

A big thing with introducing yoga to children is to have an element of make-believe.

We like to pitch it to their level, and use lots of animals, characters, and other 'real' things to illustrate the poses.

A lot of the yoga moves we're about to look at are 'real' poses, but they are re-branded to make them child friendly. This taps into children's interests and imagination better.

So, for example, the classic 'half moon pose' becomes the 'superman pose.' This is much easier for children to visualise, and it also really motivates them to want to give it a go.

1. Superhero Yoga Poses

Here are some excellent poses to try out the first few times you try yoga with children. All of these superhero poses develop strength, boldness, and power.

Brave Superhero Pose

This is the standard 'warrior pose 1'. Step forward into a lunge position, and reach both arms up over your head.

Hold this for a few seconds. Then stand back up and repeat a lunge with your other leg.

Brave Superhero Pose

Strong Superhero Pose

This is officially know as 'warrior pose 2.'

Lunge forward again, hold the pose, and lift both arms out at your sides. Look over the fingertips of one hand first, then switch your head and look over the fingertips of the opposite hand.

Peaceful Superhero Pose

Lunge forward, and then hold the pose with your back straight. Reach one arm down to your back leg, whilst your front arm reaches up to the sky. This one is a bit harder!

Hold the pose for a few seconds, and then repeat on the other side.

Superman Pose

This is classically known as the 'half-moon' pose. This is much trickier (just to warn you).

Start in the lunge pose again with right leg forward, and bring your right hand down to the floor in front of you whilst lifting up your back leg.

Stretch out your arm on top to the sky. Good luck!

2. Imaginary Trees

Trees are a popular choice for child-friendly yoga.

Most children have experienced trees, and understand how they stand, move, and are rooted to the ground. All these features can be imitated through yoga.

This is a movement activity combined with visualisation.

Ask the children to stand tall like a tree. Put their feet together, and their arms by their sides.

Take two deep breaths, close their eyes, and ask them to focus on their feet. Imagine them being rooted into the ground like the roots of a tree.

Encourage the children to feel their roots growing from their feet into the ground.

Then get them to imagine this growth spreading upwards through their bodies. Ask them to lift their arms, and put them out wide like branches.

A simple yoga tree

Now imagine there is some wind. Their arms will sway like branches. Imagine the wind getting stronger, which increases the movement. Swing your arms from side to side, swaying backwards and forwards.

At last the wind will stop. Become aware of the stillness, experience the balance, and think about how you feel.

3. Animal Poses

One of the easiest ways to teach yoga poses is linking them to different animals. Some of the classic poses already have animal names, such as 'downward facing dog.' With others, you can link the position to an animal with just a bit of imagination (such as 'giraffe pose').

Seal Pose

Lie flat on your belly. Put your hands on the floor near your head, and push upwards until your arms are straight.

Your legs will still be on the floor, but your upper body will be raised, with your back curved.

Seal pose

Giraffe Pose

Stand with one foot in front of the other. Raise both arms together as high as you can go. Stay like this for a few moments, then slowly circle your arms downwards until you try to touch your feet. Once again try to hold, before repeating.

Giraffe pose

Downward Facing Dog

The idea of this is to make an upside down 'v' shape with your body. With your hands on the floor in front of you, and feet also on the ground, push your midriff up into the air. Your back and legs should be straight, with the corner of the 'v' your mid-section.

Downward facing dog

4. Moving Animal Poses

Turtle Pose

Lie on your back, and then make your body into a ball by pulling up your knees to your belly, and hugging your legs with your arms.

Now you are going to try to rock backwards and forwards like a turtle in a shell. This acts like a kind of relaxing back massage.

Fox Pose

The children go in a plank position, only with knees on the ground. They raise one arm and the opposite leg upwards until they are level with their body. Then they put them down, and raise the other leg and arm.

Keep going like this.

5. Animal Poses With Sound Effects

Although it's not the traditional way to perform yoga, some of the animal poses can be combined with some sound effects. This is particularly good for really young children starting off their yoga journey.

Snake Pose

The children lie on their bellies. They put their arms behind their backs, and try to raise their head and shoulders off the floor.

Go, '*ssssss!*'

Frog Pose

With feet on the floor and shoulder-width apart, crouch down, with your hands on the floor in between your feet. Make a noise like a frog – '*rebbit, rebbit.*'

Frog pose

Lion Pose

Kneel on the floor, and put your hands down, with arms straight, so that you are on all fours. Put your head up high, curve your back, and roar!

6. T-Rex Eyeball

This is a great game for any dinosaur enthusiasts out there.

Get something that will be the 'T-Rex Eyeball'. Something like a pebble would be good, or a rubber spot.

Place this 'eyeball' on the ground in front of the children.

The children are going to look at the object, and try to balance on one leg.

The T-Rex can't see them if they don't move. It's as simple as that.

Looking at an object really helps them to balance, and it also helps focus and mindfulness.

7. Qigong – Beachball Breathing

Although not strictly yoga, we thought we should add a couple of Qigong activities to this chapter.

Qigong is similar to Tai Chi. It is a series of slow and controlled movements, that are performed for their relaxing and meditative qualities. Practitioners claim it to have similar health and mindful benefits to yoga.

This beachball breathing activity is a simple one to start with when getting started with Qigong.

The children stand with both hands together and facing up near their bellies.

The children are going to imagine they are holding a giant beach ball in their arms.

Beachball breathing

They are going to move their hands around the imaginary sides of the beachball until they reach the top, near the children's heads. As they do this they are going to breathe in.

Then they are going to push down from head to tummy with their hands, breathing out as they do it. They are imagining that they are deflating the beach ball.

Then breathe in, and inflate it, once again moving their hands around the ball up to their heads.

Keep inflating and deflating it, with arms moving in a circular motion before going straight back down.

8. Archer Pose

Here's another relatively simple Qigong pose that's great for children.

Stand with your legs wide apart, with one leg straight and the other bent. Now you are going to pretend to fire an arrow. Hold an imaginary bow in one hand, and pull back the pretend arrow with the other.

Archer pose

As you pull back the arrow, breathe in. Then you are going to push the arrow forward through the bow, breathing out at the same time. The hand that was the bow, is going to pull back at the same time.

Then repeat – load the bow up, breathing in as you pull the arrow back. Repeat several times.

7

Mindfulness And Movement

You've probably noticed how children like to move! It is definitely the natural way of things.

Many people associate mindfulness with stillness, especially for adults.

However, mindfulness and movement can definitely be combined, and in fact *should be* where children are concerned.

Here is a simple formula that definitely seems true for at least some children:

Movement + Mindfulness = Greater engagement

Combining mindfulness and movement will have excellent results.

Also, mindfulness is partly a process of self-realisation. You start to understand how your body and mind work.

These games we're about to look at are really good for understanding our bodies. How do our bodies work? How do they react to things? How do they feel at different times?

These games are all physical, with lots of movement involved. They contain many benefits, such as:

i) Children learn to move in different ways
ii) They root children in the present
iii) They develop simple listening and attention skills
iv) The games encourage excellent cardio exercise

The central theme of all the games is that children are thinking about how their bodies work.

Allow for periods of activity, and then periods of calm. Use these calm times to focus on different things, such as their heart beat or physical sensations.

These games are also fun (woop!), and promote mental health and happiness.

1. Noisy Running

This is a really crazy one to warm up with! But children really love this game.

Basically the children are going to be moving in different ways, and they will be making noises that are connected to their movements. When they walk, they make a really quiet noise. When they jog they make a louder noise, and when they run fast they make the loudest noise they can!

Any kind of noise is fine. Something like 'arrgh!' is the standard.

The adult's role is to support and encourage them.

It's a good idea to start off quite structured with this. Ask them to walk (with quiet voices).

Then jog. Then run!

Flip between the different movements.

The loud running is really liberating, and is a moment of letting everything go.

You can have a mindful moment after the yelling. Signal for them to stop in some way, and ask them to close their eyes. What does their heart feel like? How does their body feel?

When children are good at coordinating the different noises with the associated speed of movement, you can try a period of 'freestyling' where they decide how fast to run and how noisy to be themselves. This is pure liberation personified!

2. Heartbeat Statues

This is a very simple concept. It is a bit like musical statues, but with an element of mindfulness thrown in.

Have at least two different types of music – one slow and beautiful, the other more hectic and fast-paced. You could potentially have several types of music (if you are able to flit between them quite quickly.)

Put the slow music on, and encourage the children to dance to it in a languid and relaxed manner. At any given moment, turn the music off, and the children are going to freeze and feel their hearts. How do they feel?

Then put the fast-paced music on, and encourage much more energetic dancing for a while. When the music goes off this time, what do their heart beats feel like?

How do their heart beats change from the immediate moment after the fast music goes off, to half a minute later?

Continue to switch between the two types of music. You can also extend the activity by trying out multiple types of music in one session.

This concept of feeling your heart-beat can be thrown into many different movement games.

3. Eagle Flying

There are several great imaginative ways of combining breathing and movement.

This 'eagle flying' game is fantastic for this. The children are going to be flying around slowly, pretending to be eagles, and gracefully beating their arms ('wings') up and down.

You breathe in when your wings go up, and out when your wings go down.

Pretending to be an animal is fantastic for visualisation and becoming fully involved in the activity. The beating of the arms really supports the deep breathing and enhances the relaxation effects of this activity.

4. Animal Dancing

This is another game that is all about letting go, and releasing pent up feelings.

Choose one child to be the 'leader', or potentially an adult could take this role. The leader is going to pick an animal, and tell everyone what they have selected. Then they are going to demonstrate how to dance about like it.

For example, they might be a monkey – beating their chest, going ‘oo oo oo’ and running about on all fours. The others copy! It’s all about really going for it.

Then the leader will try a different animal, and the others copy.

The adult could ask questions to try to extend the types of movement.

Have a go with a few different leaders.

It’s nice at some points for everyone to sit down and close their eyes. These moments of calm are a super thing to add to any movement game.

5. Eye Openers

This ‘eye openers’ game really brings the wonder of how your eyes work to the forefront of children’s attention.

We use our eyes every waking moment. In mindfulness, we particularly use them to take mental snapshots, study objects and notice changes.

This adult-led game helps children to practise using their eyes.

It is a sequence of eye exercises that you model and the children try to copy.

Some great exercises include:

i) Look up, look down, look left, look right (without moving your head)
ii) Make your eyebrows dance – both of them together

iii) Can you do one eyebrow at a time?
iv) Can you blink slowly?
v) Blink very fast
vi) Roll your eyes
vii) Open your eyes wide
viii) Close your eyes
ix) Open your eyes just a crack
x) Look at your finger in front of your face, and then look at something really far away

To conclude the activity, all close your eyes. What do you 'see' when your eyes are closed?

6. Superhero Heartbeats

This is a game that combines mindfulness with superheroes and missions.

The children are all superheroes that have different abilities. Tell them what the abilities are and how to pretend to do them.

For example, some good ideas are:
Fly – they soar around with arms out
Bounce over buildings – jump around
Shrink – crawl around
Freeze – stand still on the spot

The adult shouts out an ability, and the children all perform it, moving around the space.

At any given moment shout, 'Freeze!'

The superheroes will stand still on the spot. This is the perfect opportunity to encourage them to feel their heart beat. How does it feel?

You could adapt this game for different animal movements, or just different moves in general. For example, if it was animals, you could move in the following ways:

Snake - slither
Kangaroo - jump
Horse - run on all fours
Owl - fly around

7. Floating Balloons

This is a beautiful and calming game. It is best played over a wide area.

Get the children to stand on the spot and close their eyes. They are going to pretend that they are turning into balloons.

Ask them to imagine how light they feel. What colour would they like to be? Imagine their skin is turning to rubber.

Then take a deep breath in, so that the balloon is fully inflated.

Then the children are going to open their eyes, and start 'floating' around the space. Model how you think a balloon might move if any of them are unsure.

They can very gently bounce off walls. The whole experience is all about floating and bouncing in a calm and ethereal way.

8. Shake And Smile

You may have seen videos of hippies in the sixties trying out things like this at music festivals! This activity is a great way of releasing tension and feeling great.

Stand on the spot to start with. Begin by gently wiggling and shaking your legs.

Then shake your legs and hips. Progress onto shaking your stomach, shoulders, arms, and head as well. As you keep going you can shake everything more forcefully. You can also start moving around, giving everything a good old shake.

It really helps if you smile as well. This releases extra endorphins. Grin, close your eyes, and shake!

After they've been doing it for a while, ask the children to stop, close their eyes, and think about how they feel.

9. If You're Happy And You Know It!

This is a way of adapting the classic song (*If You're Happy And You Know It*) to incorporate different emotions and ways of moving that relate to those feelings.

Always finish with the happy verse at the end to lift the mood!

Here are some examples of verse lyrics with actions:

'If you're happy and you know it...'

Clap your hands
Smile
Thumbs up
Shout 'Hooray!'

'If you're angry and you know it...'
Frown like this
Stamp your feet
Shout 'No!'

'If you're sad and you know it...'
Cry and cry
Mooch about

'If you're tired and you know it...'
Yawn real wide

If you're excited and you know it
Go 'Yippee!'
Cheer and shout!

This is a good song for acting out what emotions look like in real life. Great for self-realisation, and understanding how our bodies respond to feelings.

10. Shoulder And Head Rolls

This is a classic relaxation technique, that combines breathing with simple movements.

Having good gross motor control in your shoulders also extends to developing smaller movements of the hands and fingers.

Start with the children standing in a space. Practise a few deep breaths to begin with, in through the nose and out from the mouth.

Then the children try to 'drop' their shoulders, and roll one forward three times, whilst still breathing deeply.

Then roll the same shoulder backwards.

Repeat this movement, forwards and backwards, on the other side.

For the head rolls, slowly drop your head down so that you are looking towards the floor. For a few moments feel the 'weight' of your head.

Then gently roll your head to one side, then back to the centre, and then repeat the other way.

8

Worry And Anxiety

All children have anxiety and worry in their lives. Unfortunately some are more or less overwhelmed by this all the time.

In this chapter we're going to look at some strategies to approach how to manage worry and anxiety.

A lot of these ideas are based around the idea of focusing worry on a physical object. You pour your anxieties into a concrete *thing*, and then that object has a way of making the worry disappear.

This technique is also used a lot in psychology – talking out the problem can capture it. This is a great way of release.

Also, lots of childhood worry and anxiety is *irrational.*

It is not really based on any logical threat.

A child might think, as a random example, that the Big Bad Wolf lives in the local park.

If children can talk about their worries, then they will slowly start to understand that this can be the case. These worries are not as big as their minds are turning them into.

These games are not about teaching children that anxiety and worry do not exist. Of course they do, and real problems are a part of all our lives.

Rather, these games are about bringing worries out into the light, and this helps children to manage and process these causes of stress.

1. Worry Box

Some kind of interesting looking box is required for this. You could use an old picnic hamper, or wooden crate, or whatever else you can find. You could even use something like a cardboard box decorated in some way.

That is the box that is going be fed with worries.

Now all you need is something to put in the box. It could be something as simple as pebbles.

To introduce the box in an adult-led game, the children sit in a circle. Give each one a pebble (or something similar like a wood slice, leaf, or whatever else).

Get the children to close their eyes, and hold their pebble in one closed hand. Imagine that whatever worry you have is going 'out' of you and into the pebble.

Then they open their eyes. One at a time, go around the circle. Everyone contributes an idea if they can, and then puts the pebble in the box.

At the end, the box is closed, and the worries put somewhere to be taken away.

In future sessions, you could revisit old worries. See if children remember what they said, and is that something that still worries them? Often it might be a recurring worry, but going through processes like this will hopefully highlight many worries as being more insignificant than they previously thought.

Older children can write their worries down on pieces of paper and then put them in the box.

We have heard of a psychologist who recommends that the children then open the box the next day and read what their worries from the previous day were. If it is something they are still worried about, then they put the piece of paper back in the box. If they are not anxious about that any more, then they rip the paper up and put it in the bin. The worry is gone!

2. Homemade Stress Balls

There are all sorts of weird and wonderful ways of making DIY stress balls.

Probably the easiest is to use socks.

Pick socks without any holes in, as even a small opening will allow lots of spillage from your stress ball.

Then you are going to get something to put inside the stress ball. Some good options are:

i) Rice
ii) Dried beans (such as haricot beans)
iii) Lentils
iv) Playdough

We'd just use one of these, so take your pick.

Pretty much all you do is fill the sock with whatever you are using, and then tie the end securely with either string, a pipe-cleaner, or something similar.

Our hands and wrists are extremely complex. There is a huge network of nerves and muscles that are interlinked. By repeatedly squeezing a stress-ball, these nerves and muscles are given a kind of work-out.

This both relieves stress, and also strengthens these areas.

3. Happy Place Meditation

This is a relaxing meditation, that can help children to be positive when facing anxiety.

Make the scene as relaxing as you can by putting on some peaceful music, and maybe dimming the lights if this is possible.

The children sit in a space, and they close their eyes.

You are going to make up a meditation that gets the children to imagine their own individual 'happy place'. Try to start with, 'Imagine you are...'

The meditation could go something like this:

'Imagine you are in a really happy place for you. You are in somewhere you love to go. All your favourite people are there. Imagine what it is all like.'

Get the children to think about the following things:

i) What sounds can you hear?
ii) What does it smell like?
iii) How do you feel when you are there?

Then tell them that you can go back to this happy place in your mind whenever you want. All you need to do is touch your finger and thumb together, and you can go back there.

Enjoy the happy scene in their minds for a few more moments.

Then open their eyes. Show them again how to touch their finger and thumb together, and then they are able to mentally go back to that happy place.

4. Mini Worry Dolls

This is a fantastic idea that comes from South America.

You have a little figure that is the 'worry doll'. You can buy little figures for this, or the children could make their own.

Small worry doll figures

The smaller the better for the dolls, so that they can easily be hidden in a box, or put in someone's pocket.

If the children make them, then they could use something like the following:

i) Create bodies from craft sticks, with faces drawn on in pen, or bits of material stuck on for clothes

ii) Use a clothes peg (pin) body

iii) Use a small pebble with a face drawn or painted on

iv) Use a small stick with things tied onto it

Anything like that will work great.

When you have your doll, there are many things that you can do with them. Some of the best include:

Worry Doll Circle Game

This is a great way to start off. Everyone sits in a circle with their mini worry doll in one of their hands.

Ask the children to close their eyes, and they are going to think about something they are worried about. Imagine that the worry is leaving you, and going into the worry doll.

Then the children open their eyes. Pass round a basket, and one at a time the children put their doll into the basket.

If they are able, the children could say their worry before putting it in. For young children, just the act of putting it in is fine.

Put Them Under Your Pillow

This is the traditional way that they are used in South America.

If a child has a worry, they put the doll under their pillow when they go to sleep.

In the morning, the doll will have sucked the worry out of the child's mind, and it is gone.

Sail Them Away

One nice idea is to make little boats for the worry dolls. Let them sail away with all your worries – across a water tray, or even a puddle.

Keep Them In Your Pocket All Day

They can suck up any worries as you go.

5. Large Worry Dolls

The larger worry dolls are a fantastic resource for shared group talk about anxiety.

They are also a brilliant fine motor exercise.

The simplest way to make them is to use a big stick, and lots of differently coloured material such as wool. Wrap the wool around the sticks. Gluing googly eyes on is also an optional enhancement!

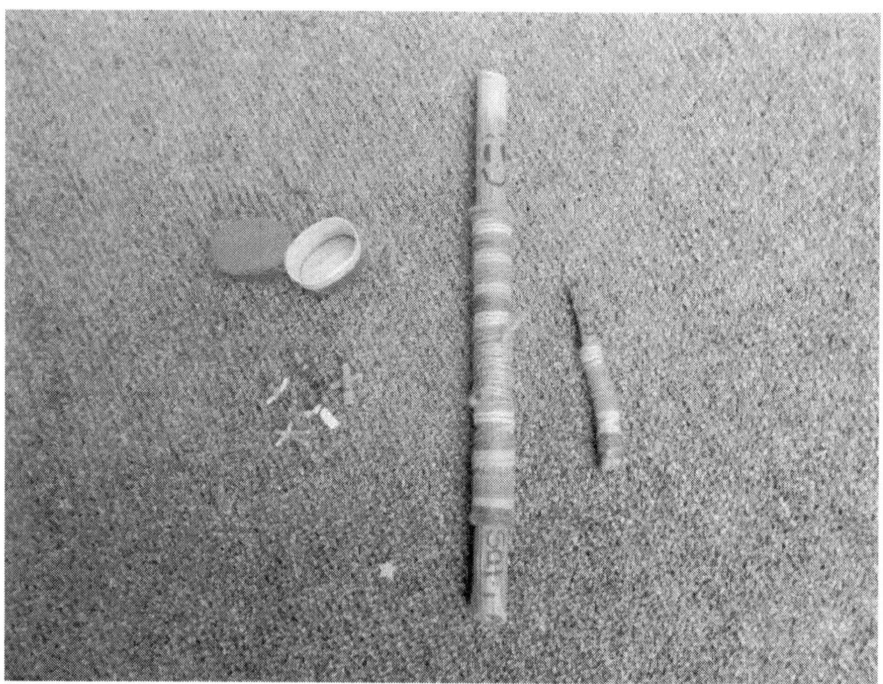

A selection of worry dolls – small, medium and large

Use these big worry doll sticks at circle time. Pass them around, and every child tries to express something they are sometimes worried about.

6. Worry Meditation

Guided meditations are a fantastic way of firing up children's imaginations. They also help them to manage their feelings.

To start with get the children to sit in a space and close their eyes. They could even lie down.

Put on some relaxing music. All try breathing deeply a few times.

Then begin with a meditation.

You could make up pretty much anything, but you want to basically stick to one of two structures:

i) The child's worry is going to get put somewhere and then it goes away

ii) Or the child is taken away from the worry

An example might be this:

'Imagine you are sitting in the park. You have a big worry. Think what that is.

There is a giant box there. The worry goes into the box, and you close the door.

Suddenly a magic carpet comes down. You get onto the carpet and fly away into the sky. You fly higher and higher, and when you look down the box with the worry in is only a tiny dot below.'

Meditations like this are not there to get children thinking that bad things don't happen in life. They are to encourage them to step back from their worries, and see them from the outside for a few moments. This really helps them to manage their feelings much better.

7. Worry Monsters

A worry monster is a really child-friendly concept.

It is brilliant for all children that love posting things (hint – all children).

The idea is that you make some kind of monster out of something like a box. The monster will have a slit mouth that you can post 'worries' into.

The children can design their own monsters with a few recycled boxes. They could paint them, or stick resources to them. Help them with the slit mouth if required.

They could post in lots of different things including:

i) Leaves
ii) Wood slices
iii) Small pieces of paper
iv) Petals

Encourage the children to think of their worries whilst holding an object. Then post it into the monster's mouth. The worry is eaten, and gone for good.

Worry monsters are great to use in an adult-led context to start with.

Sit in a circle, and give out one object to each child (for example, some leaves). Get them all to first think of a worry, then pass the worry monster around. The children say their worry, and put the object into its mouth.

You can later explore using worry monsters in more child-led situations.

9

Massage

Massage is something growing in popularity in many schools around the world.

This is fantastic news, as it is just what modern children need – a way of reducing stress, developing mindfulness, and also encouraging cooperation.

There are two types of massage that we can use - *peer massage*, which is where the children massage each other, and *self-massage*, which is where the children massage themselves.

Peer massage is done fully clothed. It is normally done following a set routine.

First, create a relaxing atmosphere. Dim the lights and put on peaceful music.

Pair the children up with a partner. The session will be split in two, the first half being when one child will massage their partner, and the second half for when they basically swap roles.

Before starting, ask the children to agree to being massaged by the other.

This is just so everyone feels secure in the partnership, and is OK with the experience of being touched by the other.

Self-massage is a simpler kind of process. Create a peaceful environment, and then the children simply perform exercises on certain parts of their bodies.

There are many benefits to massage. It is a deeply relaxing experience, and of course:

Relaxed = happy + ready to learn

Also anything that relieves stress will help enhance concentration.

Stress deeply undermines concentration. It produces adrenalin, and parts of the brain start shutting down. Massage counteracts this, and opens out the neural circuits ready for more holistic thinking.

Massage is also a very social experience. Children get to interact with others in a positive way. It is great for bonding, and for forging friendships with others.

To get the maximum benefits for massage, it is a good idea to do it pretty regularly. Every session will involve a few different exercises.

1. Peer Massage (Shapes)

There are lots of very simple massages that children can carry out on each other. Many of these involve 'shapes'. If the children know a shape that they are trying to draw on a certain part of their partner's body, then it makes the process really easy for them to understand.

Here are some great ones to try:

Hearts

You start with your hands on either side of your partner's spine, about half way up their back.

Draw a 'heart' shape, by pushing up and round towards the shoulders, before sloping down to the start point.

Repeat this movement several times.

Hearts

Spectacles

With two flat hands, make circles around the shoulder blades several times. These are the circular frames of the spectacles. Then push out in a line towards the shoulders (those are the legs).

Repeat this process.

Butterfly

Start with two hands flat in the middle of the chest, either side of the spine.

Make a clockwise circle with the right hand, followed by an anti-clockwise circle with the left. This motion draws a butterfly shape.

Butterfly

2. Peer Massage (Movements)

Here are some simple peer massage techniques that have a simple imaginary movement as the main exercise.

Brush The Horse

Start with one hand near your partner's head and stroke down the side of the spine to near the bottom of their back.

Then stroke down the other side of the spine with your other hand, once again starting near their head and progressing to the base of their back.

Kneed The Dough

This is a classic 'shoulder massage'. The children put their hands on their partner's shoulders, and squeeze them gently, like a ball of dough.

Bear Walk

Put your hands on either side of the spine, near the base of the back. The child's hands are the bear's feet. Walk them slowly up the other child's back.

Bear walk

Ice Skating

They put their hands on either side of their partner's spine. The children move their hands up and down the back. When one hand is going up, the other should be going down, and vice versa.

Ice skating

3. Raining On Your Head

This activity is a great way to begin with self-massage.

Pretend it's raining. The children are going to make a pitter pattering action with their fingers. Encourage them to gently let their wiggling fingers touch their head, imagining the rain is landing in their hair. Continuing with the pitter-patter fingers, they can go down their face, their neck, shoulder, arms, belly, legs, knees, onto their toes, and all the way back up.

Raining on your head

Imagine how wet you are.

Then brush all the 'water' off you with your hand.

Imagine the sun coming out and drying you off. Close your eyes and feel the warmth of the sun. Take several deep breaths, enjoying the sun's heat.

4. Hand Massage

Self-massage can be an excellent source of stress-relief. It also helps us connect with our bodies.

Some really simple exercises to start off with hand massage include:

i) Simply shaking your hands gently

ii) Gliding your index finger and thumb along the fingers on your other hand, going up and down one finger at a time

iii) With your thumb, making circles on the heel of the other hand

iv) Making circles with your thumb in the palm of the hand

v) Stroking the back of the hand with your fingers in a circular motion

5. Foot Massage

This is best done in bare feet.

It is also easiest to be seated in a chair. Ask the children to bring one of their feet up on to their opposite thigh.

Some great starting points for foot massages are:

i) Ask them to make their foot and ankle as floppy as possible, and give their foot a good wiggle

ii) Massage the whole foot with your thumb. Move along the foot from the heel, across the arch, to the toes and then back

iii) Hold each toe and circle it a few times one way, and then a few times the other way

iv) Stroke each toe from the base to the nail and back

v) Stroke the top of the foot with the fingers, back and forwards or in a circle

6. Pressure Points

Simple massaging of some key pressure points is another good stress reliever.

Before you start, it's good for the children to be calm, and to have taken a few moments doing some kind of breathing activity (see the Breathing Games chapter).

Head

This is the simplest pressure point massage.

Have the children try to put their pointy finger on the spot in between their eyebrows. Then close their eyes, and circle their finger gently on this spot for a few moments.

Ear

There is a pressure point in the top part of our ear. It is at the apex of the triangle hollow. This point can help ease anxiety and stress, as well as having positive benefits for sleep.

Finding it is the difficult bit with this activity. It is good to do it as a partners activity, with your friend helping you find the correct bit of your ear.

When found, do the same gentle exercise on it, circling your pointy finger.

Hand

There is a pressure point in between the index finger and the thumb. It's basically underneath the webbing in this part of the hand.

Put your pointy finger on this area, and gently circle.

Quick safety tip – this area is supposed to be linked with labour, so pregnant staff should avoid demonstrating this exercise.

10

Visualisation Games

Mindfulness helps us engage fully with the present.

It is about cutting through the distractions, and being involved completely with whatever it is that you are doing at that time.

Visualisation games are a fantastic way of training the mind to be completely present.

Visualisation is quite simply imagining something strongly. It is a bit like guided day-dreaming. Children strongly imagine things that are happening, guided by a game, or the words of an adult.

Here are some spectacular visualisation games, and many contain other elements like relaxation, deep breathing, or simple movement.

1. Magnetic Hands

This is a simple gentle movement game, combined with deep breathing. It is calming and relaxing, and helps children to focus on one thing.

The children stand or sit in a space. Practise a few deep breaths together first, breathing in through their noses, and out with their mouths.

Ask the children to put their arms in front of them at shoulders width apart, with their palms facing each other.

Now for the visualisation bit. The children are going to imagine that there are powerful magnets in the palms of their hands, and they are attracting strongly together.

Slowly the children will bring their palms almost together, whilst breathing in through their nose (the hands don't actually touch – leave a small gap). Then they breathe out through their mouths, as they bring their hands back to where they started at shoulder's width apart.

Keep going like this, going in and out, whilst breathing deeply at the same time.

2. Melting Mindful Moments

The idea of this game is that you are going to visualise being something that melts.

So you could be a snowman on a warm day, or a bar of chocolate in the sun.

The children stand in a space and close their eyes. They imagine (as an example) that they are a snowman. They start to feel the warm sun beating down on them.

They can feel their bodies start to melt and sink downwards towards the ground.

Start crouching downwards towards the floor. In the end, the children will have fully 'melted' and be lying on the ground.

Take a few moments to breathe deeply, and just savour the experience.

3. Throw Your Troubles

The children stand or sit in a space and close their eyes. They hold out one hand in front of them.

Encourage them to imagine something they are worried about. Ask them to imagine that the worry is sitting in the palm of their hand.

They are going to close their fist and really crush that worry! Squeeze all the life out of it, and then throw it away into the air.

Imagine it flying away into the distance, or vanishing in the sky.

Ask the children how they feel.

4. Sky Floating

The idea of this game is that the children imagine they are different things that are floating about in the sky.

This is really brought to life a lot more if you include a moment of calm before they 'turn' into each different thing.

To start off, everyone stands in a space, and closes their eyes. Imagine they are turning into something that floats. Some good things to try are:

i) Clouds
ii) Feathers
iii) Birds
iv) Planes
v) Leaves falling from trees

As an example, let's imagine they are going to transform into feathers.

With their eyes closed, encourage the children to visualise that their body is slowly turning into a feather. Imagine their bodies turning all soft and fluffy, with the hard spine running down the middle.

Then the children open their eyes, and begin to waft around the room. Model how to move like a feather, slowly, floating from side to side, going up and down, spinning, and all that kind of thing.

After a couple of minutes, everyone stops and closes their eyes one more time.

Imagine another transformation.

Some ways to move include:

i) *Clouds* – Imagine how light and fluffy you are. Float around, blown by the wind
ii) *Birds* – Soar, flap their wings, swoop
iii) *Planes* – With arms out take off, do loops, land
iv) *Leaves falling from trees* – flutter, sway, waft from side to side

5. Meditation Flying

This is a beautiful cool-down exercise for the end of a structured physical education session. It is also a way of combining stillness with imagination.

Ask the children to lie down on the floor and close their eyes. The children are going to imagine themselves becoming lighter and lighter.

At last they are going to lift up off the floor and start floating around the room.

They fly out of the window, and begin flying over your local area. What can you see?

You can either let the children speak and offer ideas, or just imagine their own thoughts in their minds.

Suggest places they might go. These could be:
i) Local landmarks that they know
ii) Their house
iii) The local park
iv) Fly over the school or setting. What can they see?
v) Fly over famous landmarks they might know – like the Pyramids, or the Empire State Building

They could go on a world tour, soaring over the Earth.

Then at last, they fly back in through the window, and settle back down on the floor. Then the children wake up.

Have a few deep breaths to finish off, and then they open their eyes.

11

Literacy And Mindfulness

As you will probably have picked up from this book already, making progress with mindfulness will help children think more clearly. This in turn will lead to greater progress across all curriculum areas – numbers, literacy, science, and everything else.

However, we're now going to take a look at just one area – literacy.

There are definitely some mindful activities that feed directly into an understanding and love of some key literacy skills.

It's now time to dive into some games you can try that will develop some of the following skills:

i) Vocabulary acquisition
ii) Turning our thoughts into words
iii) Talking about the impressions of our senses

1. Positive Word Bag

For children to think in a positive way, they will need language to vocalise their thoughts.

Creating a 'kind vocabulary' can be done by creating a resource of kind words that are presented in some sort of child-friendly way.

So, for example, you could set up a bag of 'kind words'. These could be written on small wooden slices, for example. They could also be written on pebbles, or wooden building blocks.

Positive word stones

Some examples of words could be the following:

· Strong
· Brave
· Bold
· Kind
· Special
· Mindful
· Calm
· Shine
· Sparkle
· Gentle
· Patient
· Focus
· Considerate
· Embrace

There is always an element of intrigue and drama whenever something is revealed from a bag! Children could take out an object, and either read the word or have it read to them (depending on their age).

Ask them things like, 'Who do you know that this word reminds you of?' 'What have they done?'

Older children can also link a resource such as a positive word bag to books that they know. They can use the pebbles or wood slices as part of small world play.

This vocabulary can also be integrated into the setting daily by the adults. The more focused and vocabulary-rich the praise that the children receive, the more strongly they develop their positive sense of self.

2. A Kindness Tree

This is probably an extremely well-known strategy, but one that has tremendous value.

The basic idea is to have some kind of 'tree'. This could be:

i) Some branches sticking out of a pot of pebbles

ii) A branch secured to a display board

iii) Some kind of 'pretend' tree made of paper or something similar, on the wall

It could, potentially, be something like a 'Kindness Basket' and just don't bother with the 'tree' element.

Either way, the main principle is the same.

A kindness tree is something that is used spontaneously throughout the day, where the opportunity suddenly presents itself. You have something to put onto the tree, such as:

i) A card

ii) A leaf-shaped piece of paper

iii) Something as simple as a sticky note

Whenever you spot an act of kindness, make a big deal of it, and write the child's name and the act down on your method of presenting.

Then attach it to the tree.

The more verbal praise you give out the better, and the more children become aware of how much these positive acts are valued, hopefully the more kindness will spread around the setting.

As an example of an act of kindness, it could be this one: 'Martha helped Liang with his zip on his coat outside.'

Put it on the tree and celebrate the moment.

You could do something similar by any of the following:
i) Writing a child's name on a pebble and putting it in a basket
ii) Write something on a wood slice

Celebrate these moments at the ends of sessions, or at the start of group times such as reading a story.

3. Proud Cloud

A 'proud cloud' is a similar idea to the 'kindness tree', except the focus is actions that make people feel proud.

Have some way of displaying the 'proud cloud'. It could be a board, a branch, or a simple cloud template.

It is good to have one in a shared area, that parents will have access to as well. For example, if you have a hallway where the children are dropped off, this would make a good place for the 'proud cloud.'

Messages for the cloud can be written by anyone.

It could be parents or carers, who have seen their child do something new at home, like go to sleep with the light off.

If could be added to by teachers or practitioners. The children could draw (or write) their own ideas about themselves or their friends.

Some tips for setting up and maintaining an effective 'proud cloud' system include:

i) Be consistent. Keep adding to it at regular intervals
ii) Promote it to parents
iii) Talk with the children about it regularly

4. Storyteller Meditations

This is a beautiful storytelling exploration, with a strong element of mindfulness thrown in.

Get the children to lie on the floor and close their eyes. Then you start a story.

For example, it might begin, 'One day, the magical fairy flew through the forest. She saw an evil witch sneaking into a cottage.'

There are many ways to continue.

The simplest is for the adult to just continue the story, and the children imagine it all with their eyes closed.

However, if you have children that are more experienced with making up stories, the next step is to nominate someone to continue the story telling. So say something like, 'Yuri, you're next.'

They try to continue the chain of events. Then nominate someone else to keep it going.

You could potentially do this as a pairs activity, with one child starting the story, the next child adding the next part, and keeping going like that. That is realistically for children from about 6 upwards, who already have some experience of confidently making up stories.

The eyes closed part really helps with relaxation and mental visualisation.

5. Get To Know Me Jars

This is another simple idea, that just requires some kind of jar, and some preparation ahead of time.

You need some kind of questions that you will put in the jar. These will hopefully be simple questions, that will get children to open up about personal preferences.

With young children, these will be read by the adults. For children that are able to independently read, they can be written in phonetically decodable language that is age appropriate.

Some examples of questions could be:

- What is your favourite colour?
- What is your favourite food?
- What is your favourite ice cream ?
- Do you have any pets ?
- What is your favourite toy ?
- What is your favourite song ?

Questions for a 'Get To Know Me Jar'

These jars can be accessed at different points of the day, and are perfect for times like 'Snack Break' or on a rainy day. The adult's role is to support the conversation.

Having something as simple as a glass jar just adds an element of curiosity and intrigue to the activity.

12

Mindful Art And Crafts

There are many adults that engage in arts and crafts for the mindfulness benefits they produce. They weave, colour, knit, embroider, make pottery, or create things with wood or metal.

Often these are hobbyists who enjoy the process above all.

The same is true when we engage in similar activities with children.

To be truly mindful, the *process,* not the end product, is all-important.

This is similar to the classic mantra of 'the process is more important than the outcome.' This is one-hundred per cent the case where mindfulness is concerned.

The important things when engaging in mindful arts and crafts are the *experience* of creating, and also the *moment* of creation.

Here are some arts and crafts that link brilliantly to mindfulness.

1. Drawing Around Bodies Meditation

This beautiful activity mixes art, mindfulness and stillness.

You either need pens and some massive paper like wallpaper for this, or you could do it on the floor outside with chalks.

The children are going to be in pairs for this game.

One child out of each pair is going to lie down on the paper or the ground (whichever you are using). Ask those children to close their eyes. You could put relaxing music on.

The other child is then going to get either a pen or chalk, and they are going to draw the outline of the other child, tracing around their body.

Then when they have finished, swap roles.

As well as encouraging stillness, this activity makes children aware of how our bodies are created.

2. Colouring Nature

Many people, both adults and children, enjoy colouring-in as a therapeutic and mindful exercise.

Of course, there are all sorts of fantastic sheets that you can print out that aid this process.

However, colouring in paper is not for everyone.

There are also many different things in nature that you can find to colour in.

Some great examples are:

i) Large leaves
ii) Wooden logs
iii) Wild flowers
iv) Sticks

Children enjoy following the natural lines in different objects. It really teaches them to experience these textures.

The important thing is what to use on them? Normal pens and pencils don't really work. The best thing to use is probably oil pastels. They seem to be able to colour on pretty much any natural surface.

Children can also try painting all of the above objects. Here's a painted leaf, for example:

Colouring and painting leaves, logs and sticks is really therapeutic

3. Happiness Scrapbook

Scrapbooking is a beautiful way to document happy memories.

It could be of time spent with friends, days out, Christmas...these photos or drawings make us smile and remember how we felt in that moment.

Scrapbooks are great for developing a feeling of gratitude for our lives. They may also help us when we are feeling down, reminding us of happier times.

An easy and quick way to make a scrapbook is to create a big one for everyone. These can be filled quickly, and provide value pretty much straight away.

Alternatively, you could have one scrapbook per child. Then this becomes more of a long-term effort.

Whichever way you do it, the scrapbook can be contributed to in the following ways:

i) Engage parents and carers to send in things from home

ii) The children can create pictures, messages, and anything else they want to stick in

iii) They can take pictures of people and things that are important to them

iv) Bring in things like tickets, postcards, and mementos of their life outside the educational setting

4. Mindful Glitter Jar

This is quite a well-known resource, but it feels like a selection of arty mindulfness activities would be kind of missing something without it. Mindful glitter jars are one of the all-time great activities.

To make a glitter-jar you need the following ingredients:

· A jar or plastic bottle

· A jug of warm water

· Some glitter glue

· A few drops food colouring

· A tablespoon of glitter (approx)

Add the warm water to the jar until it fills about three quarters of it. Then pour in the glitter glue, and mix it with the water.

Put in some drops of food colouring and stir.

Pour in the glitter!

Then top up the jar with warm water so that it is almost all the way to the top. You just need a little gap at the top to help the mixture move and shake around.

Screw on the lid, and you are ready to go.

The idea is that the children shake the jars, and then watch the swirling patterns. They are good for helping relaxation, and also simple mindfulness.

5. Puddle Art

This one can get a bit messy, but it's a beautiful way of using puddles for learning.

There's different ways of doing it.

To start with you need some kind of puddle, so it's clearly great on a rainy day. You could get a palette of paint, and try swirling the paint through the puddle with brushes.

Puddle art

Another way is to squirt the paint directly into the water (not for the faint of heart).

In the end the puddles will almost always go brown, but up to that point there are all sorts of opportunities to observe the fantastic swirls and effects of paint and water combining.

6. Making Lava Lamps

We'd definitely only do this activity adult-led, to avoid any oil spillage catastrophes.

Have a jar with a lid, and oil of some sort for this. Any oil will work – baby oil, vegetable oil, corn oil, or whatever else.

To start with, take the lid off the jar, and fill it about halfway up with oil.

Have some pots of water with a bit of paint mixed into it.

Use pipettes to suck up some of the coloured water and drop it into the oil in the jar.

It will create all sorts of mysteriously coloured blobs on the surface of the oil. Squirt hard, and the paint will go deep into the oil before floating upwards.

You can put the lid on the jar and shake it, observing the effects that happen from this. Just make sure those lids are on tight!

There are other things that you can add to this jar to make different visual reactions. Bubbly tonic water will be an interesting addition, for example, sending multiple bubbles through the oil and paint.

7. Drawing in Malleable Substances

There is something simple and powerful about drawing with fingers straight into substances.

Sand is great for this. You can draw pictures into it, or create patterns or shapes.

Other substances include:

i) Shaving gel
ii) Porridge oats

iii) Gloop

As well as all the mark-making children get from this, there is also the experience of touching and manoeuvring the substance. Draw the children's attention to what sensations they feel. What does it feel like on your finger?

8. Giant Drawing Or Painting

There is something very liberating about either drawing or painting on a big scale.

This is a very simple concept. Provide some kind of huge surface, such as:

i) Bed sheets on the floor or hung up on walls
ii) Huge wallpaper
iii) Massive chalkboards on the ground or floor
iv) Walls
v) Sheds or fences painted with chalkboard paint

Draw (or paint) straight onto the surface. Encourage freedom of expression and big movements.

9. Messages On Seed Paper

Seed paper does exactly what it sounds like it should do – you can grow seeds on it.

This magical paper can first be decorated by the children. They could do any of these things (depending on their age):

i) Draw pictures of things that are important to them

ii) Older children can write messages to friends or loved ones
iii) They could draw pictures of their friends and family
iv) Draw a place that means something to them
v) Draw a memory

Plant seeds on the paper, and watch the shoots grow over the next few days and weeks.

10. Mandalas With Mirrors

Mandala activities could be pretty much a whole book by itself.

Mandalas are symmetrical assortments of shape and colours.

A loose parts mandala

One of the best ways for young children to start with them is by using 'mirror books.' This is a very simple idea. You get two safety mirrors and tape them together, so that they can open out like a book.

Stand them up on a table, or on the ground, so that they are roughly open at about 90 degrees.

Then you put something inside the mirror book. Whatever you put in will be reflected multiple times in the mirrors, creating a gorgeous mandala.

Using mirror books is probably the easiest way to create mandalas

Some great things to put in include:

i) Leaves
ii) Petals
iii) Stones
iv) Shells
v) Corks
vi) Bottle tops
vii) And pretty much any other type of small loose part

There are lots of things going on at the same time. There is all the curiosity and 'awe and wonder' that the activity generates.

There is also a lot of mathematical concepts going on. There is symmetry, and it is also a visual introduction to multiplying.

If you put the mirror faces much closer together, you are able to multiply the image many times over. Put them much wider, and you only get a few reflections.

11. Snowflake Mandalas

This is another simple way to get started with mandalas, and begin to appreciate their qualities.

Have some circles of paper that have been cut out before starting the activity. Fold them over into eighths, and then cut out snowflakes, by snipping into them with scissors.

Open them out.

Then you can do all sorts of things to add colour to these mandalas, such as:
i) Lay them on paper, and colour in between the holes
ii) Paint them
iii) Draw and colour on them
iv) Scatter glitter over them, then lift them up, seeing the symmetrical patterns left underneath

13

Exploring Senses

It's been very hard condensing the hundreds of activities that focus on our senses into just a handful for this chapter.

However, in the end we've just picked a few simple but highly effective games...

1. Listening To A Bell

This is a really simple idea to get started with. This idea is used in Buddhist meditation.

This game is an easy listening game, combined with mindfulness.

Have some kind of bell, or another instrument that is able to produce a long, sustained sound.

All you do is ask the children to be silent and then ring the bell.

Listen to the noise of the bell dying away until it is gone.

You can try these variations:

i) The children put their hand up until they can hear it no longer (when they put their hand down)

ii) They mimic the noise of the bell with their mouths

iii) Find other objects that have a long noise, and listen to them

2. Texture Bags

What could be simpler than compiling a few objects with very different textures and putting them into a bag?

You can then use the texture bag in a range of ways, including:

i) Simply putting your hand in and exploring

ii) Making up stories with the objects

iii) Have objects that link to a book that they know

3. Adding Scents To Materials

There are all sorts of objects that can be infused with different smells.

This generates talk, and also really gains children's sense of curiosity.

Some ideas include the following:

Playdough

It is very simple to add things like vanilla essence, or lavender to the recipe for a beautiful infused smell.

Small World Play

Mini herb bushes or garlands added to small world areas as pretend trees offer both an imaginative and a sensory experience.

Sensory Bins

Mix some interestingly scented objects in with other random things to be explored by young fingers.

Smell Bottles

You simply need some kind of bottle or jar for these. Fill them with water, and something that has an interesting smell.

Water Play

A couple of drops of something that smells interesting added to water play makes it a much more multi-sensory experience.

4. Imitating Instruments

Instruments of course have unique sounds, tones, and timbre.

Luckily, though – so do our voices!

We can easily try to copy the sounds of instruments by humming, moaning, screeching, and wailing along.

This is best done first in a very structured way. The children sit in a circle. Have a selection of a few simple instruments to start with – for example, a drum, a triangle, a tambourine, and a bell.

The adult plays one of these and the children try to mimic the sound.

So, if it's a triangle, they might make a noise a bit like '*ting!*'

You can adapt this game in lots of ways, such as some of the following:

i) Play a repeated rhythm on the instrument, and get them to copy the noise

ii) A child makes the noise of one instrument (with their mouth), and the others try to guess which one it is

iii) Try some kind of 'band' of instruments – with children making different instrument noises at the same time (this is a very much harder game!)

14

Connecting With Emotions

Learning about emotions in others helps children to learn more deeply about themselves.

It also teaches empathy, and connects children more strongly to those around them.

Here are a collection of fun emotions games, that teach a whole host of skills including cooperation, emotional intelligence, and self expression.

1. Power Of A Hug

There is probably no greater emotional balancer than a hug.

This 'power of a hug' activity is a very beautiful and simple game.

Have children move around a space. Call out a number. Whatever the number is, that is the number of children that are going to hug each other in groups.

If you call out, '1', then the children hug themselves. They give themselves a squeeze with their eyes closed.

Call out '2', then hug the nearest person to you.

Call out, '3', then get involved in a team hug of 3, and so on. Children can also hug in groups of 4 or 5.

This is a great team-bonder and icebreaker.

2. Hugging Games

There are all sorts of well-known games that can be adapted to include hugging.

Some examples are:

Hug Relay

Do a normal type of relay race, but instead of handing over an object or tagging your team-mates, give them a hug at the change-overs.

This is probably best done with slower races to avoid injury. For example, it could be a jumping race, a hopping one, or moving like an animal. Hugging at full speed is not recommended!

Musical Hug

This is a bit like musical statues. Dance around, but when the music stops, hug the person next to you.

Pass The Hug

Sit in a circle. The first person hugs the child next to them. They hug the person next to them, and the hug is passed like this around the circle.

3. Emotion Jars

This is a fun craft activity, that can also be used to illustrate how our minds work.

If all the children are making one, you need one plastic jar each, water, glitter, beads, shells, and whatever else you would like to fill the containers with.

Pour water into the jar, add whatever 'ingredients' you like, and then screw the lid on.

Emotion Jar

Sit in a circle with the jars.

Explain that these jars are like our minds. When we have too much going on, our minds go a bit like this...shake your jar!

Everyone shakes their jar, and watches the snowstorm effect.

Explain that if we stop for a few moments and are calm, then our minds can start to be still again.

All leave the jars on the floor without touching them, watching the objects settle.

4. Don't Laugh Or Smile

This is a fun game that is a great friendship builder.

The children sit in pairs. One child is going to be trying to make the other one laugh or smile.

They are going to use all their best tricks – silly faces, funny jokes, noises, impressions, and all the rest of it. The other one has to resist smiling or laughing.

This game helps children to think about how they can control their reactions and facial expressions.

You can extend the game with some mindful questions. Ask things like, 'How did you feel when you smiled or laughed?'

5. Weather Feelings

Learning to compare your feelings to the weather can have positive benefits.

Just like the weather, feelings cannot be fully predicted.

Also, feelings and weather are continually changing. Moods come and go like clouds. Bad weather passes, as do negative feelings.

For this 'weather feelings' game, get the children to close their eyes. They are going to think of something that makes them happy.

They are going to breathe in, and then breathe out sunshine into the room.

They are going to fill the room with light, and the sky will turn a spectacular blue.

You can also try the same for other emotions, such as sad or angry.

For example, everyone thinks of something that makes then angry. This time imagine your are breathing out a terrible storm. Fill the whole room and then the world outside with black clouds, thunder and lightning. Keep breathing it out until there is no storm left in you, and the whole thing is out of your body and in the world around you.

If you try breathing out 'sadness', then you can fill the sky with dark clouds.

After trying out one of these negative emotions, it is definitely a good idea to finish on a positive, and visualise happiness again. Fill the room back up with beautiful sunshine.

6. Expression In The Mirror

This is a classic emotions game, that has withstood the test of time.

Give each child a small safety mirror, and then explore different facial expressions whilst looking into them.

For example, try the following faces:

i) Make a long face
ii) A tiny face
iii) Puff your cheeks out
iv) Suck your cheeks in
v) Eyes almost shut
vi) Eyes wide

vii) Mouth open wide
viii) Mouth pursed tight

Talk about how your faces feel as you try these out.

Then move onto emotion faces. Try some of the following:
i) Happy, sad, angry
ii) Scared, surprised, disappointed, worried (all of these are depending on the age of the children. Start with the easy vocabulary and concepts first).

Ask the children about how pulling the faces makes them feel. Do the faces remind them of any experiences - places, feelings, or people?

7. Pairs Emotions

The children get into pairs for this one.

They sit facing each other. One child is going to be the 'leader' to start with, and the other is going to copy them.

The leader makes different faces, and the other child tries to copy them like a mirror. They try different emotions. It's good if the child copying can try to name how they are feeling as well.

They could also try silly faces, or unusual faces, animal faces, or anything else that they can think of.

This activity is a great building block for developing empathy.

Have a go of lots of different faces, and then change roles.

8. Emotions – Hide Your Mouth

This is a fun variation on the pairs emotions game.

One child is the leader to start with, and the other child is going to be doing the guessing.

The leader does some kind of emotion face (e.g. happy, sad, angry), but covers their mouth as they do it with their hand so that it is hidden to the other person. That child will try to guess which emotion their friend is doing.

Children will start to see that there are other clues around the face that can help you understand how another person is feeling.

For example, there will be movements in the cheeks, around the eyes, and sometimes the forehead depending on the emotion.

9. Do What I Say, Not What I Do

This is a trickier pairs emotions game, which is for children from about five upwards.

One child is the leader, and the other child has to try to do what they say.

The leader will try to do one emotion, but say another one for their partner to copy. As an example, they might say, 'Do a happy face,' but then do an angry one. Their partner has to do what they say, not what they do (e.g. do a happy face).

This is a fun game of trying to trick your partner, whilst also thinking about emotions.

10. Face Collages

This takes a little preparation to set up.

Find lots of faces of people in magazines (or photocopied from books), and cut them out. Ideally they will be faces of people showing a range of different emotions.

Cut the heads in half horizontally about level with the base of the nostrils.

The game for the children is to make different faces. Use different upper and lower halves of the heads, and talk about what the faces look like.

It's a fun game of experimentation, and making funny looking characters all showing different emotions.

11. Emotion Art

This is extremely open-ended and can be achieved in a range of ways.

The idea is to use different media to portray an emotion.

Emotional music of some sort is great for this. It could be classical, or some other form of music that strongly suggests a particular way of feeling - happiness, sadness, anger, terror, or whatever else.

Put this music on, and explore whatever media it is. This could be tried with painting, drawing, collage, or creating marks in messy substances.

15

Mindful Brain Activators

The idea of some of the games in this chapter is doing something a little *odd.*

Our lives are made up of multiple actions that we repeat over and over, and we become accustomed to performing them in a certain way.

We develop patterns of behaviour.

We do the same actions, in the same order, again and again.

Breaking up this sequence of actions with something out of the ordinary can really get us thinking. Try brushing your teeth in a different way, or carrying out your morning routine in a different order.

These experiences connect us to the present.

They get us thinking about what we are doing in the here and now.

1. Mindful Mixing Up Routines

This is a simple thing to try out during the many routines of a typical day.

Whatever action children are currently engaged in, throw in a suggestion of how to do it differently.

So, for example, if they are putting their coats on, can they try putting their other arm in the sleeve first? Can they zip their coat with their other hand?

An activity like this may sound almost trivial, but it really gets them engaged with the present.

2. Crossing The Midline Aerobics

You have almost certainly heard of the midline before.

The simple idea behind this is that there is an imaginary line that runs vertically down the centre of our bodies.

Young children work well symmetrically, with this midline as the line of symmetry. So, when a toddler waves one hand, they will often wave their other in a symmetrical way.

Any physical activities that help children cross this midline with their limbs is beneficial to mindfulness.

Cue 'Crossing the Midline Aerobics'!

Put some pumping music on, and then you are going to model some great moves that cross this central line.

Repeat each one at least four times to the beat of the music, with the children copying.

Some good moves would be things like:
i) Pointing across your body to one side
ii) Pointing with your left finger into the air on the right side of your head (and repeat with the right finger)
iii) Touch your right foot with your left hand

And any other movements that you can think of like this will help a huge amount.

3. Pennies Game

Like all the best mindfulness games, this requires some super simple resources – namely a handful of pennies, cents, or whatever else your currency is. You also need some kind of basket to put them in. It is best to use coins that look a bit 'different', i.e. different ages, colours etc

Give one penny out to each child, and get them to look at their penny. Give them at least half a minute to do this.

Then ask them to all put their pennies into a basket.

The idea now to pass around the basket of pennies. The children will try to take out just 'their' penny.

When they have got out the one they think is theirs, they will also try to explain why.

This game gets them problem solving, and applying critical thinking.

4. Slow Motion Walking

This is another game that disrupts the children's normal way of doing things, and gets them thinking as a consequence. It is also good for relaxation and deep breathing.

Go on a walk as a group outside. Whilst walking, try going in 'slow motion'. Lift your feet and breathe in, and then place your foot down as you breathe out. Continue like this, slowly moving their legs as they breathe deeply.

5. Walking Over Different Substances

This is another really simple activity.

It is best done outside. It throws into focus the experience of walking over different materials, and all the sounds, textures, and potentially smells that this conjures up.

You could set up some different materials on the floor, but much easier is to just go out and find some.

As a group try walking, slowly and deliberately, over crunching sticks, dry leaves, squidgy mud, over pebbles, over logs, and on whatever else you can find.

Ask lots of questions and try to get them to really savour the experience.

You get all the wonderful vocabulary out of activities like this, such as mud that is slurpy, gloopy, splatty, splodgy, and all the rest of it.

16

Mindful Nature

Nature offers all sorts of mindful opportunities.

There are the wonderful smells... sights... textures... growth... transformation....

All in all, a fantastic melting pot of experiences that have a positive impact on our thoughts and feelings.

1. Growing A Herb Garden

All the senses are involved in the growing of herbs. You get all the fantastic smells, tastes, and sights.

You can grow herbs in a variety of different containers.

Some good ideas include:
 i) In tubs screwed to pallets or a fence
 ii) Fill tyres with soil and plant herbs
 iii) In jars

iv) On shelves
v) Out of cups

One way to incorporate mindful crafts into this experience, is to get the children to create clay pots. These could be painted, or decorated with clay knives, and then used as herb planters.

The beauty of herbs is that they are extremely resilient (always a bonus when young children are involved). Also they are quick to grow.

Some good herbs to try include rosemary, thyme, dill, parsley, mint and edible flowers.

2. Hole Punch Magic

Cheap hole punches are a fantastic thing to use on leaves, and also on petals.

You can get hole punches that create differently shaped holes – moons, stars, trees, and all sorts of other silhouettes.

These are great for fine motor, as well as really helping children experience the colours, textures and smells of leaves and petals.

Some ways of using the hole punches include:
i) Making patterns
ii) Hang the leaves from clothes lines. The sky will shine through the holes on a bright day
iii) Shine torches through the leaves in a dark den or box
iv) Make 'confetti' ideal for stirring into potions
v) Fine motor activities you can try with the 'confetti' – e.g. picking up bits with tweezers

Hole punches and leaves

3. Leaf Weaving

These leaf weaving activities develop out of the beautiful hole punch ideas above.

The children basically get some leaves, and punch some holes in them.

Then you are able to try some of the following weaving ideas:

Leaf Strings

This is probably the simplest leaf weaving game. A child will have one long piece of string. They thread leaves with holes in them onto the string, making a long chain.

Weaving One Leaf

This is a beautiful weaving activity using just one leaf.

Have a leaf with many holes all over it that the child has created with a hole-punch. Weave coloured string through the holes, in and out, creating a random weaving pattern.

Making Mobiles

This is a cocktail of the two above activities. Weave materials through the leaves, and then put them all in a string.

The leaf strings can be hung from branches, or from the ceiling.

4. Flower Perfume, Soup, And So Much More

Engaging the senses creates memories. It helps our brains become much better at processing information.

Flowers have a huge sensory impact on our minds.

Get some fresh flowers, and there are all sorts of fantastic potions you can create. These include:

Flower Perfume

Mix petals in water. Add all sorts of gorgeous substances like glitter to make it look even prettier!

You could also add things that changed the smell, for example, vanilla essence, or herbs.

Flower Soup

This is the good old-fashioned mixing up of lots of petals with water, and whatever else you can find – conkers, leaves, grass, and all the rest of it.

Flower Magic Stew

Stir up water and petals in a pot. Cast spells, chant, and laugh like real wizards and witches.

Mashed Flower Paste

Put lots of petals into a pestle and mortar. Have a go of squishing the flowers.

Bashing them a few times will release the wonderful odours.

If children are skilful at the squishing process, then they can in theory turn the flowers into a kind of mushy paste.

5. Flower Sensory Trays

This is a dry-based flower activity.

Have lots of petals or flower heads mixed up in an assortment of other dried substances. Something like rice, lentils, or beans would work well.

You can do lots of things with this sensory tray:
- i) Use tongs to get the flowers out
- ii) Pour and tip the substances with ladels, spoons, and other containers
- iii) Swirl it with paint brushes or spoons
- iv) Create writing patterns, or form letters or numbers

6. The Simplicity Of Fresh Flowers

This is a very simple and mindful activity.

Provide a large bunch (or several bunches) of fresh flowers.

Place them in some kind of bowl or vase.

Children can try any of the following:
- i) Flower arranging! Experiment with colours and form
- ii) Snipping petals with scissors
- iii) Drawing their arrangements

7. Creative Colours

For this you need some kind of glass jars or bottles, some food colouring, and some kind of flowers.

Fill the jars or bottles with water, and add food colouring.

Place the flowers in the coloured water, and observe them over the next few days as they start to absorb the colour.

It works really well with white flowers, like carnations, or even daisies that the children can pick themselves.

8. Flower Sticks

There are different ways of creating these. The basic idea is that you attach flowers to sticks in some of the following ways:

Journey Stick

Go on a journey, such as around the park. Whatever you find, put it in a bag (things like leaves, petals, nuts etc).

Then, when you get back, attach what you found to a stick. Use wool to twist around the objects and firmly attach them to the wood.

These sticks are good for retelling experiences.

Mark-Making Sticks

Using rubber bands, attach flowers to the ends of sticks. These are great for painting with, dipping the flowers in paint, and printing on large paper.

Magic Wands

Find sticks, and lots of things to put on them (leaves, petals etc). Then twist wool and other materials around the sticks, securing the items to them.

17

Final Thoughts

It's time to take a huge mindful breath as we have reached the end of the 101 games.

We hope this has been a beneficial insight into the wonderful and simple world of mindfulness and wellbeing.

By popular demand, we have created a 'Cheat Sheet' to go with this book. It is basically all 101 games on a single handy piece of paper, perfect for putting on the wall as an aide memoire. The cheat sheet can be found at https://earlyimpactbooks.com/happy-cheat/

If you have enjoyed this book, we would be so grateful if you could leave a review on Amazon. These reviews really help to promote the book to a wider audience, and spread the impact that these ideas can have.

We would also recommend checking out our online program, 'Happy Minds Academy.'

This is the ultimate step-by-step video course that shows you how to set up an outstanding mindful culture in your school, nursery, or daycare setting.

There are five modules, covering everything you could possibly need to know:

Module 1 - An overview of mindfulness - statistics, facts, research, benefits

Module 2 - Setting up an outstanding mindful environment

Module 3 - A full toolkit of mindful activities to inspire learning across the whole curriculum

Module 4 - Systems to engage the parents / carers, and embed the mindful culture

Module 5 - How to maximise staff wellbeing

We also have a customer's only online facebook community to go alongside the course, where those that enrol can ask questions, share successes, and engage with others on their mindfulness journey.

To check out the online course, then go to https://earlyimpactlearning.com/happy-minds-academy/

All that remains is to wish you all the best if you try any of these ideas out!

Mindfulness can have such huge benefits. It can help children relax, and learn at a much accelerated rate. Even more importantly, it is a crucial skill that will serve them well throughout their lives.

THE END

P.S. Please remember to download your free book if you haven't done so already. You can find it here: https://earlyimpactbooks.com/50-games/

Your Free Book Is Waiting

Also by Martin Williams and Kelly Sheils

Other books available from Amazon include...

101 Games To Play Whilst Socially Distancing
The Amazon #1 Bestseller.

Attempting social distancing with young children raises many questions.

Split into 12 areas of the curriculum, this book offers 101 scintillating games to play in the context of social distancing for children aged 3-7.

Reviews

Rosie on Amazon

I have been on several of Martin's courses...and been blown away by all the ideas and suggestions he has for Early Years. This book is no different!! Superb!
Rosie, Review on Amazon

I am so excited about this book!! This book is a GODSEND. It is so well written and well structured, so easy to read... I wholeheartedly endorse it. Such a handy resource!!
Sunshan, Review on Amazon

Squiggle, Fiddle, Splat! 101 Genius Fine Motor And Early Writing Activities

Early education teachers have a major problem on their hands – many children just aren't interested in anything to do with fine motor or early writing any more.

The number of children with fine motor difficulties is increasing year on year. Teaching early writing becomes harder and harder with every passing day. So, what can we do?

Read this book to find out all the answers, and particularly to learn how to provide games that are scintillating...inspiring...alluring...that are strongly tapped into the interests of the children, and are something they cannot resist!

Review

What a fabulously practical resource!

If, like me, you have accumulated a pile of 'teaching books' that you never get around to reading- buy this and put it straight to the top of your list. READ IT STRAIGHTAWAY!

Helen Dillon, Review on Amazon

Loose Parts Play - A Beginner's Guide

Looking to unleash the powerful learning potential of loose parts play, but don't know how to begin...

Loose parts play offers a magical and wonder-filled way to deliver learning across the whole curriculum. But there are many things you need to know to get started on the correct footing (and many things that will go wrong if you don't)...

Bursting with more than 200 practical ideas, activities and provocations, this is the perfect guidebook for anyone looking to develop an outstanding loose parts curriculum either at work or at home.

Reviews

I particularly like that this is a child-led approach and that the resources are simple everyday objects. It is great to see the imagination and creativity it encourages in our pupils - this is the reason why most of us entered the profession. This is a brilliant book and I will be digesting its ideas for some time.

Gregg, Review on Amazon

Excellent insight into loose parts play. Accessible for both teachers and parents, lots of inspiring ideas and examples. Wish I had read this for my children! Would highly recommend.

Nicky L, Review on Amazon

101 More Games To Play Whilst Socially Distancing
The bestselling sequel.

101 more imaginative games to help children stay happy, healthy and learning in the 'new normal.'

This book is an amazing sequel to 101 games to play whilst social distancing. I have been trying out different games with the children I teach (Nursery-Yr1). There are some lovely games for promoting well-being and discussing emotions with children which has been invaluable in this uncertain climate. A great book and an amazing resource for any classroom.
Candice, Review on Amazon

Once again, another well thought out, imaginative set of games to add to the armoury. This book, along with its predecessor has a myriad of engaging and inspirational games which hold the attention of the players with no difficulty at all - a winner on all counts when my job is made easier! Highly recommended for all types of educator and parents too!
Mrs C M C Ashby, Review on Amazon

Printed in Poland
by Amazon Fulfillment
Poland Sp. z o.o., Wrocław